Everything You Need to Know About

A DRUG-ABUSING PARENT

A drug-abusing parent causes many problems in a family.

Everything You Need to Know About
A DRUG-ABUSING PARENT

Frances Shuker-Haines

THE ROSEN PUBLISHING GROUP, INC.
NEW YORK

Published in 1994, 1997 by The Rosen Publishing Group, Inc.
29 East 21st Street, New York, New York 10010

Library of Congress Cataloging-in-Publication Data

Shuker-Haines, Frances.
    Everything you need to know about a drug-abusing parent /
Frances Shuker-Haines.
        p.   cm.
    Includes bibliographical references and index.
    ISBN 0-8239-2613-3
    1. Children of narcotic addicts—United States—Family relationships—
Juvenile literature. 2. Narcotic addicts—United States—Family
relationships—Juvenile literature.   [1. Drug abuse. 2. Parent and child.]
I. Title.
HV5824.C45S54 1993
362.29'13—dc20
                                                                93-32182
                                                                    CIP
                                                                    AC

Manufactured in the United States of America

Contents

Introduction

Being a teenager in today's world can be very difficult. Problems with school, friends, and peer pressure can leave you confused and in need of support. It's important that you feel you can rely on your parents for the love and support you need. Your parents should be there to help you understand the world around you.

Sometimes, however, a parent may have many problems of his or her own. Sometimes a parent may turn to drugs or alcohol to escape these problems. When a parent is a drug or alcohol (substance) abuser, he or she has an illness. Your parent is sick, just as someone with cancer is sick. Your mother or father needs help.

Living with a parent who is abusing drugs or alcohol upsets your family and your life. It's important for you to

Many over-the-counter drugs and prescription drugs can become
addictive.

know that you are not alone. Millions of teenagers in the United States live in families that are affected by substance abuse. These substances include alcohol, cocaine, heroin, crack, marijuana, depressants, and stimulants.

The Children of Alcoholics Foundation reports that there are 28 million children of alcoholics in the United States. Seven million of them are under eighteen years old. No matter what drug your parent is abusing, the effects on you and your family are destructive and painful.

This book will help you recognize substance abuse. It is difficult to admit that your parent has a problem with drugs or alcohol. Ask yourself the following questions. If you answer yes to five or more of them, your parent is most likely a substance abuser:

1. Do you often wish your parent would stop using drugs or alcohol?
2. Do you worry about his or her health due to drugs or alcohol?
3. Does your parent fight a lot when he or she is high or drunk?
4. Do you cry and/or feel sick because of your parent's abuse?
5. Do you ever have to protect yourself or another family member from your substance-abusing parent?
6. Does your parent often break promises because of substance abuse?
7. Are you embarrassed to invite friends over because of your substance-abusing parent?

8. Do you wish your family was more like your
   friends' families where there is no drug problem?
9. Do you ever think about running away from home?

You may not remember a time when your parent did not abuse drugs or alcohol. It may be all you know. It's important to realize that your parent's behavior is not normal. It is not the way most parents behave. It is not the way most families function.

All teens should have a safe place to live. You may feel guilty about your parent's abuse, but it is not your fault. You have done nothing wrong. You have done nothing to cause your parent's drug problem. You cannot fix your parent's drug problem. But you can do something to take care of yourself and to make your life better.

Reading this book is taking the first step. It will tell you what you can and can't do to help your parent. Most importantly, it will tell you what you can do to help yourself. It takes courage to take action. Be proud of yourself for taking this step.

A person addicted to drugs has a constant need to satisfy the addiction.

Chapter 1

Drugs and Drug Abuse

First, let's discuss what drugs really are. Drugs are any kind of substance that makes your mind, your mood, or your body feel or act differently than it normally would. Some drugs are good—they can make sick people well, or ease the pain of people who are badly hurt.

You may have taken acetaminophen, cough medicine, or cold medicine. These are drugs that are available over-the-counter at a drug store. They are safe if used properly. You may also have used penicillin or other antibiotics. These drugs are legal and safe when used correctly and prescribed by a doctor.

But sometimes people take prescription drugs for non-medical reasons. These drugs include depressants, such as barbiturates or benzodiazepines (downers). Depressants slow down the heart rate and pulse. Your parent may abuse the drug by taking larger amounts or by using it for a longer period of time than is directed by the doctor. Or they may take them just to get high.

Alcohol is legal for people who are over twenty-one years of age. But alcohol is a drug, and adults can abuse it if they don't control their drinking.

Some people abuse drugs that are illegal. These drugs include narcotics, such as heroin; stimulants, such as crack and cocaine; and hallucinogens, such as LSD, Ecstasy, and marijuana.

Some people are able to use drugs and alcohol without becoming abusers. But many people cannot. Abuse often leads to tolerance. Tolerance is when a person needs more of the drug to get the same effect. An abuser will consistently increase the amount of the drug they are abusing.

At this stage, people become physically and psychologically dependent on the drug. When someone is psychologically dependent, it means they think they need the drug in order to function. Being physically dependent means the body actually needs the drug in order to function. To be physically or psychologically dependent on a drug results in addiction.

When someone is addicted to drugs, he or she has little control over the abuse and cannot stop without help. Here are some of the ways you can tell if someone has a drug/alcohol problem.

A drug abuser:
- cannot stop using or drinking
- turns into a "different" person when she or he is using the drug
- makes excuses for using drugs ("I had a bad day at the office . . .")
- tries to cover up his or her drug use, or pretend it "isn't that bad"
- forgets things that happen while she or he is high or drunk
- won't admit that she or he has a problem.

Not every substance abuser does all of these things, but most of them do at least one or two of these things. Trust your instincts. If you feel that your parent's use of drugs is a problem, then it is. Teens shouldn't have to worry that their parents are doing something unhealthy or illegal. If your parent's use of drugs makes you uneasy, scared, or angry, then your parent is abusing drugs and needs to stop.

How Did This Happen?

You might wonder how your parent became a substance abuser. That's not easy to answer, because the reasons are different for each person. Here are a few reasons why your parent may have become a substance abuser:

Some drugs are very addictive. Your parent might have tried crack or heroin a few times to be sociable or out of curiosity. He or she may have enjoyed the way the drug made him or her feel. Without meaning to, your parent may have become addicted. Now your parent's body "needs" the drug to avoid having painful and often frightening physical symptoms.

Substance abuse tends to run in families. Your parent may have had a parent who was also a substance abuser. Some studies show that children of substance abusers are at a higher risk of becoming substance abusers than children of parents who don't abuse drugs or alcohol.

Tragedy. Sometimes bad things happen in life. Some people turn to drugs or alcohol to help them get through a hard time. They may take drugs to help numb the pain. They may take drugs to keep feeling "up" when life is getting them down. The problem is that drugs can't solve problems. They only make more problems.

An accident, a disease, or a physical ailment. Some people become addicted to prescription drugs. These are drugs that are given to people by doctors to help them get well or feel better when they are sick. What starts out as help gets out of control and turns into abuse.

Try to remember that no one means to become a drug addict or an alcoholic. Your parent is sick. He or she deserves a chance to get help. Everyone deserves a drug-free life—including your parent and you.

Chapter 2

How Drug Abuse Affects Your Parent

Abusing drugs or alcohol will change many things about your parent. Your mother or father may behave strangely toward you. Your parent's mood may change quickly and without warning. He or she may tremble or shake because the body is strongly affected by addiction to drugs or alcohol. Watching your parent become angry or depressed can be scary.

Jennifer's Story

Jennifer knew her father was changing, but she didn't know why. She could see that he was losing weight and seemed to be nervous all the time. He was coming home late from work quite often. Jennifer helped her mom make dinner. They would save a plate for her father, but he was never hungry.

"I ate at the office," he would say. Jennifer didn't believe him—he wouldn't be getting so skinny if he wasn't skipping meals.

When her father was home, he chain-smoked at the table and laughed loudly at silly things. He didn't pay attention to what Jennifer said; he just kept talking, not making sense.

One day, her father came home even later than usual. He seemed wild and all wound up. He'd laugh and talk fast one minute, then yell angrily the next. Jennifer didn't know what to expect. For the first time in her life she was frightened of her own father.

Her father could barely wake up the next morning and he was in a terrible mood all day. Jennifer was upset, too. "What's wrong with Dad?" she finally asked. "He's so different than he used to be." Her mother sat down and explained to Jennifer that her dad had a serious problem—a drug problem. He was addicted to cocaine.

Physical Changes

Some of the bad things that drugs do to your parent are physical. Drugs such as amphetamines, cocaine, and crack are stimulants. They can make a person's heart race and, in some cases, cause a heart attack.

Stimulants, or "uppers," may also cause people to become jumpy, fidgety, nervous, confused, and aggressive. And when the drug's effect wears off, the user may become depressed, tired, and unable to care for himself or herself.

Drugs known as depressants, or "downers," (such as Valium or alcohol) slow down the central nervous system and make people feel sleepy and slow. Downers make

A drug-abusing parent's behavior can be confusing and frightening to a teen.

people unable to react quickly or to do things that require a lot of coordination, like driving a car. Downers make it difficult to think clearly. And often downers cause people to feel depressed.

When the effects of downers wear off, a user may feel sick, vomit, and become restless. Depressants can be very dangerous because if the user stops taking the drug without seeking medical help, he or she could have seizures, which can result in a coma or death.

Narcotics, such as heroin or morphine, which are strong painkillers, often have the same effects as depressants.

Drugs known as hallucinogens, such as LSD, cause people to see and hear things that aren't there. People feel as if they are dreaming even when they are awake. They often don't know what is real.

Any drug can harm your parent if it is used incorrectly. Substance abuse can damage the heart, the liver, and the brain. An abuser can die from overdoses of drugs or alcohol.

Substance abusers can also hurt themselves and others through accidents or risky behavior. Drugs can cause someone to fall down, to walk across a busy street against the light, to drive a car recklessly, or to take unnecessary chances.

Psychological Changes

We have discussed how drugs affect your parent physically. Being a drug abuser may also affect your parent psychologically and cause strange, yet somewhat predictable, behavior.

Your parent puts drug use before anything else. The drug becomes all-important. Your mom or dad is

In a healthy family, the parents take care of their children. In a family with a drug-addicted parent, you may have to help take care of your parent.

addicted to the drug—dependent on it—and cannot control their need for it. Even though your parent loves you, he or she may take advantage of you or put you in danger to get more drugs. If your drug-abusing parent does not get help, the drug will take over his or her life.

Blaming everyone else. This is typical of the "disease" of substance abuse. The abuser needs excuses to use drugs. So the abuser accuses others of making him or her drink or do drugs. "You're driving me to drink!" "You kids make me so crazy, I need a pill to calm down!" "I'd be okay if my boss gave me a chance."

Pretending that the drug problem isn't a problem. A substance abuser often pretends to "forget" the embarrassing and harmful things that happen while he or she is high or drunk. Sometimes the abuser is so drunk or "wasted" that he or she really can't remember what happened. Your mom or dad may not believe what you say because she or he is too ashamed and afraid to face the problem.

Mark's Story

Mark's mom liked to give parties. She was always inviting people over. She and her friends would make all kinds of drinks and Mark's mom would act really silly and loud. Mark hated to see her like that—it was so embarrassing.

Over and over Mark or his dad suggested daytime activities that didn't involve drinking. But Mom wanted no part of them. She said that it wouldn't be any fun. It seemed like Mom was always looking for an opportunity to drink. "Let's celebrate the first day of spring!" she'd say, and fix herself a drink. Or, "Look at Mark's great report card; he deserves a toast."

Family relationships often suffer as a result of drug abuse.

One day, Mark's family decided to go on a picnic. Mark and his dad packed a cooler with sandwiches, chips, fruit, and soft drinks. But as soon as they spread the blanket, Mark's mother started to look for a beer or a bottle of wine.

Mark's dad told her that she didn't need an alcoholic drink. He said she drank too much and should "give it a rest." She looked at him blankly and said, "I don't know what you're talking about. I'm not some wino lying in the gutter somewhere. I just want to have a little fun. What's wrong with that?"

The next thing they knew, she was heading for the car and was off to find "a little something." Mark and his dad knew she was going to get a drink. The picnic was ruined.

Sometimes Mark felt that drinking was all that his mother cared about. It was more important than a picnic. It was more important than him. It was more important than anything.

Responsibilities of Your Parent

A parent who puts drugs first is not considering your needs. A parent who is "stoned" or drunk can't make good decisions or handle emergencies. A parent who gets loud or argumentative or depressed while using drugs can be scary and dangerous. A parent who causes family problems and will not admit it is not a good role model. A parent who loses a job because of his or her drug abuse is not providing for the family.

You may feel that your parent doesn't care about you or love you anymore. You may feel that you don't

A drug-abusing parent often blames other people or events for his or her addiction.

get enough attention from your parent. Your parent is responsible for you. Although the law varies in different states, generally you are being neglected when:

- A parent fails to provide food and clothing for you;
- A parent fails to provide an education for you;
- A parent fails to provide medical care for you if he or she has the money to do so;
- A parent leaves you alone for long periods of time.

You may be very angry about the ways in which your mother or father is not a good parent. You have every right to be. You deserve parents who nurture and care for you. Unfortunately, your parent has a disease. Even though your mother or father still loves you, this disease stops her or him from being a good parent to you.

The "Disease" of Substance Abuse

In this book we refer to substance abuse as a disease. Doctors and substance-abuse experts describe it as a disease for many reasons. These are some of the reasons:

1. It follows a pattern that is the same for most people.
2. It has symptoms that are the same for most people.
3. It gets worse if not treated.
4. There is a standard (generally accepted) way to treat it.

Before doctors started calling substance abuse a disease, people thought that abusers were just "weak" or "bad." People believed that if abusers tried harder and really wanted to change, they could stop abusing drugs. Now we know that the abusers are not bad; they are just powerless to control what is happening. They need trained people to help them learn about their disease and how to stay away from drugs forever.

One way drug addiction and alcoholism are different from some diseases is that a person can get better, but he or she can never be completely cured. Drug abusers are in recovery for the rest of their lives. Being in recovery means constantly making an effort to stay off drugs. If an abuser starts to use drugs or alcohol again, even if it is only a small amount, he or she will risk becoming addicted again. If an abuser does start using again, it is called having a relapse. A relapse is a setback in recovery. Any time an abuser uses drugs again, he or she is no longer in recovery.

Thinking about your parent's drug problem as a disease may help you, too. It may help you stop blaming yourself. After all, you couldn't give your parents cancer, could you? Well, you can't give them drug addiction either. Your drug-abusing parent is truly sick, but your taking the blame for his or her problem will not help him or her.

The truth is that your mother or father never meant to be a bad parent. You may find it hard to believe, but your mother or father only wants the best for you. This terrible disease of drug abuse prevents him or her from giving you the best. The good parent your mother or father means to be is still "in there" somewhere. And, someday, if your mother or father gets help for their addiction, you may see that parent again.

Children of substance abusers usually feel confused and disturbed about their life at home.

Chapter 3

How a Parent's Drug Abuse Affects You

*Y*asmin *tried to spend as much time away from home as she could. She hated going home after school. She liked spending the afternoon at her friend Denise's house. Everything was so much nicer there. Denise's parents didn't fight all the time. Denise's parents didn't break promises because they were too drunk to remember. Denise didn't have to lie to her friends about her family.*

But Yasmin had to go back to her house eventually. Often she would find her mother passed out in the bedroom. Yasmin would have to cook dinner for her brother and father. When her mother would finally wake up, the fighting would start. When her father and mother yelled at each other, Yasmin hid in her bedroom. She would dream about running away from home. Anything, even living on the streets, would be better than this, she thought.

Having a parent who is a substance abuser is very hard.
It can make you feel sad, angry, confused, depressed,
and afraid. The main thing for you to remember is that
any way you feel about your parent's drug abuse is okay.

It's Not Your Fault

Many teens with substance-abusing parents feel
that they are the cause of their parent's addiction. They
think that if they were better-behaved children, worked
harder in school, were more helpful around the house,
or worked part-time, maybe then their parent would
stop abusing drugs. But that isn't true. You are not the
reason your parent abuses drugs. And you can't make
him or her stop abusing drugs. Only your parent can do
that—with the right kind of help.

How Teens Cope

Being angry and upset day after day is a hard way
to live. Not knowing what to expect from a drug-abusing
parent can be very stressful. Different people deal with
their feelings in different ways. Some children of
substance abusers become quiet and withdrawn. They
may have learned to be this way at home to keep a
drunk or drugged parent from getting mad. Or they
may try to keep their own anger hidden inside because
they are afraid to explode and lose control.

Other teens become loud and rowdy. They may become the "class clowns" who make up stories to shock
friends. They may be trying to let out some of their anger
in ways that don't seem so bad.

Some teens create problems for themselves and others. They skip school or break rules. They do things that are mean or harmful. These teens may be so angry they just can't control themselves. Or they feel so alone that they don't care what happens to them. Since they feel ignored at home, they try to get attention any way they can.

A drug-abusing parent in the house can make some teens take on too much responsibility. Some teens look after their younger brothers and sisters day and night. They cook the meals, do the grocery shopping, do the laundry, and may have to pay the bills. They may even be the ones to clean up after Mom or Dad when the parent has been on a binge (a period of excessive drug or alcohol use). These overworked teens try to create some order in their lives. They try to have the "normal" life their parents can't give them. But when teens take over the role of the parent, they lose a part of their childhood.

Maintaining Your Self-Esteem

Most teens who grow up with a substance-abusing parent also suffer from low self-esteem. That means they don't feel very good about themselves. They may think they aren't very important. Teens with substance-abusing parents are often put down, criticized, or abused. They begin to think they don't deserve to have good things happen to them. They think that they must be bad, or else bad things wouldn't be happening to them.

Teens may be faced with greater responsibilities if they need to take over for a parent with a drug problem.

This is not true. If your parent uses drugs, it doesn't mean you are bad. You shouldn't be made to feel that you don't deserve good things. You do. If you feel this way, keep reminding yourself that you are a good person in a bad situation. Tell yourself that you are not to blame for what is happening to you, your parent, and your family.

If You Are Abused

Unfortunately, parents who are dependent on drugs or alcohol are often abusive to their children. The abuse may happen in different ways; it could be emotional or physical. But it is always used to control another person. Some people get angry and upset easily when they drink or do drugs. They can't think clearly. Some people feel powerful. They hurt the people around them. If this sometimes happens in your house, you must tell someone about it. Talk to an adult you trust so he or she can find a safe place for you to go. It is *not* okay for your parent to hurt you. You don't ever deserve to be hurt.

Sexual abuse can be one of the most harmful types of abuse. Sexual abuse is when someone touches you on your genitals (vagina or penis), buttocks, or breasts. That person may make you touch his or her private parts, or force you to perform sexual acts. Any kind of touching that you don't like is abuse. If sexual abuse is happening in your house, find someone you can trust to talk to right away, even if your parent told you to keep it a "secret." If you are scared for your safety,

Finding a friend to confide in may help in coping with a bad family situation.

don't keep silent about it. Protecting yourself is more important than protecting a parent's behavior. It is wrong for your parent, or anyone, to abuse you, and it should be stopped.

The Cycle Continues

One of the saddest things that can happen to the children of substance abusers is that they can also become substance abusers. In fact, if your parent abuses drugs or alcohol, you are *much* more likely to suffer from the same disease than people who grow up with parents who are not addicts. No one knows for sure how many kids will become addicts, but studies have shown that 40 to 60 percent of children with chemically dependent parents will become chemically dependent themselves. Every child in this situation is certainly at risk.

Is it "genetic"? That is, do these kids inherit the disease at birth, the way they inherit eye color or hair color or the shape of their ears? That is a question that is still not fully researched. Scientists have done studies, however, with adopted children who had birth parents who were substance abusers. A lot of those kids grew up to be substance abusers, even though the parents who raised them were not. That makes scientists think the disease of drug addiction may be somewhat genetic. But further studies need to be done in order to be sure.

It is likely that growing up in an unhappy home will make you an unhappy adult. And many unhappy adults turn to alcohol and drugs for "help." This is especially true when children have grown up watching their own parents turn to drugs to solve their problems or escape from them. That's why it is so important to get help for yourself now.

You must learn new ways to help yourself and new reasons to love yourself. And that's why you must understand that you are at risk. You, of all people, need to develop healthy ways to deal with stress, peer pressure, a broken home, or any of life's other problems that you may have to face.

Many children of substance abusers grow up thinking, "It will never happen to me!" They may think that because they have seen how horrible drug abuse is, they will not get hooked. They may feel safe enough even to experiment with drugs—"I know when to stop!" But it doesn't take long before these children lose control and become chemically dependent.

One of the painful things about drug abuse is "denial." Drug abusers convince themselves that they don't have a problem when it's obvious that they do. This is another reason to be careful. Once you become addicted, you are no longer reasonable. That is why avoiding drugs in the first place is the safest, surest way to stay drug-free.

Don't hurt yourself the way your parents are hurting themselves. Don't hurt others the way you are hurting now. You can break the cycle. You can keep yourself drug-free and enjoy your life.

Children of drug-abusing parents sometimes mistakenly think that getting rid of the substance will get rid of the problem.

Chapter 4

What You Can't Control

You may wish you could make your parent stop drinking or getting high. But you can't "fix" your parent. You can't cure your parent's disease.

There is nothing you can do to make your parent stop taking drugs. Your mother or father *can* get better. Your mom or dad *can* stop being a substance abuser. But you can't force your parent into recovery. It is your parent's decision to stop drinking or stop using drugs. Only when your mom or dad admits to having a problem and gets help will recovery begin.

Codependency and Enabling

You want your life to be normal. You may sometimes do almost anything to make it seem that way. Sometimes you may try to cover up your parent's drug use to protect your younger brother or sister. You may say, for example, "Mom's just having a bad day. It's nothing to worry about." Or, "Dad was out late last night and needs his sleep this morning." Sometimes you may do work around the house that is your parent's responsibility. Or you may make excuses for the drug-abusing parent when a promise is not kept. "It's okay that you missed my game today, Mom. It probably would have given you a headache anyway."

You need to understand that you cannot rescue your parent from drug abuse. You may become preoccupied with your parent's abuse. You may constantly worry about his or her behavior and begin to tell lies to cover for him or her. You may become more interested in getting your parent to stop using than anything else. But every time you make an excuse or tell a lie, you enable him or her to keep drinking or using drugs.

By trying to control your parent's behavior, you allow the disease to continue. When you enable someone to continue his or her drug abuse, you are called codependent. Codependent means that you are so caught up in your parent's disease, you forget to take care of your own needs. Unfortunately, the only person who can get a parent to stop abusing drugs is the parent.

It is not easy to stop enabling. If your parent is abusing drugs, you are probably trying your best to get through each day. But it's time to let yourself off the hook. Stop cleaning up after your parent. Stop lying to protect him or her. Stop pretending that you aren't angry. Stop

Many children of substance abusers cover up for their parent's problem by taking care of all the chores and trying to smooth out conflicts.

trying to be perfect. Try to remember that nothing you do or don't do will make your parent stop. The only thing you can do for your parent is to let him or her suffer the consequences of the drug abuse. Drug abusers need to see what their abuse is doing to them and to the people around them.

You might feel bad about letting your parent suffer. It may seem like a selfish way to act. But in reality, you will be helping your father or mother realize that he or she has a problem and needs to get some help. This realization is the first step toward recovery.

Chapter 5

What You Can Control

I t can be hard to accept all the things you can't do in this situation. Realizing that you can't stop your parent from abusing drugs or alcohol can make you feel powerless. This chapter will tell you how to regain some control in your life.

Don't Keep your Parent's Abuse a Secret

You are not a bad son or daughter if you talk about your parent's drug problem. What is going on inside your home may be very painful and upsetting for you. There is no need to go through this alone. If you can admit that there is a problem, you have taken an important first step. You will start to feel better when you begin talking honestly and openly about your feelings. *41*

There are many people available who are ready to listen, and who can support you at this difficult time. When you decide that it's time to start taking care of yourself, you can get in touch with:

Your school guidance counselor or a teacher. These staff members are trained to help young people as they grow into adulthood. They may be working with other students who have a drug-abusing parent. Or they may be able to refer you to another professional who specializes in your kind of family problem.

Your priest, minister, or rabbi. It may be comforting to talk with someone who already knows your family. He or she will not tell anyone about your conversations but may be able to suggest other people you can contact.

A trusted relative or adult friend. A grown-up who knows you well and cares about you may be the easiest person to talk to. This person may offer the love, support, and encouragement that you have missed for a long time. He or she may also offer you a place to stay when you need to "get away" and think about things more clearly.

A friend. Millions of children are growing up in families like yours. Chances are, someone you know is going through the same thing you are. Talking to a friend can help, even if your friend's parents are not substance abusers. Friends are there to love you and let you know you're okay. A good friend wants only the best for you.

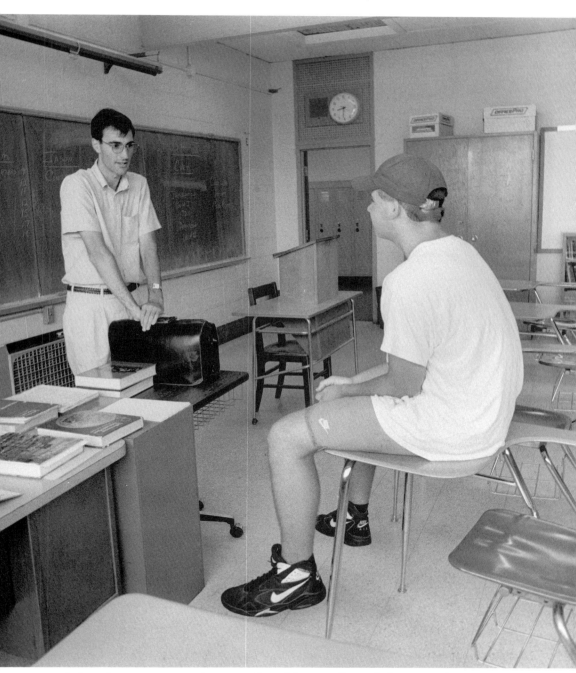

A teacher or counselor may be able to offer advice on where to get further help.

Learn More About It

Drug and alcohol abuse are complex problems. More and more is being written about their causes, their treatment, and how the whole family is affected. This book, and others mentioned in the back of this book, can explain some important things about substance abuse. The more you learn about addiction, the more you will understand your drug-abusing parent and what is happening to you. You can learn to separate yourself from your parent's problem and live your own life.

Protect Yourself and Get Help

You have a right to be safe. Anytime you feel that you are in serious danger in your home, leave immediately. Go to the house of a neighbor, friend, or relative. Or go to some other safe place. If you cannot leave, try at least to get to a phone. Call 911 and say that you have a police emergency.

Some kids are turning in their drug-abusing parent to the police even if they are not at risk. They know that many drugs are illegal and dangerous, and they want their parent to stop using. But this is a serious step for kids to take on their own. There are many things to consider. Although no one can tell you for sure whether this would be the right thing for you to do, an adult may be able to advise you.

Help is always available to young people who join *Alateen*. This nationwide organization brings together the teenage children of the substance abusers. They meet in groups to discuss their experiences and their feelings. They give each other love and support. They let each other know that they don't have to feel "different" or alone anymore. They also give each other positive ways to cope with their situation. They learn how to love the abusing parent without being codependent. Above all, they learn how to focus attention on their own lives and participate in rewarding activities.

Try to remember that helping yourself is also about pleasing yourself—being good to you. Do the kinds of things that make you happy. Work on your self-esteem. Hang out with people who believe in you. And continue believing in yourself.

The understanding and caring of friends can be a great help for teens involved in a bad family situation.

Chapter 6

How to Help a Friend

*K*atie had always been best friends with Sarah. They grew up on the same block. They shared everything and spent a lot of time with each other. They often did their homework together, and they spoke on the phone every night.

But lately, Katie has noticed some changes in Sarah. Sometimes when Katie calls, Sarah says she can't talk and just hangs up without explaining. It seems that Sarah is always in a hurry to get away from her friend. Katie is worried. She's certain that Sarah isn't doing all her homework—and that's not like Sarah either.

Sarah started making excuses why it was not convenient for Katie to come over to her house. Katie was beginning to wonder what was going on.

One day, Sarah began asking strange questions about Katie's father. Sarah wanted to know what he was "like" at home. She asked Katie if her father was ever mean. Did he ever hit her or make her feel uncomfortable in any way? Katie said no. She told her friend that her dad was a pretty nice guy. He had strict rules about schoolwork and TV, but he was kind. Sarah started to cry. Katie didn't know why.

The last time Sarah came over to spend the night at Katie's house, Katie's whole family had dinner together. Everybody was talking about their day and laughing. Again, Sarah started to cry. She ran from the table and Katie ran after her. "What's wrong, Sarah? Why are you so upset?" Katie asked. "I wish I had your family," said Sarah. "My family is just a big mess. I can't take it anymore." Then Sarah finally told her friend a family secret—Sarah's dad was an alcoholic.

Some of you reading this book may be worried about a friend. It's great to be concerned, because most kids whose parents are substance abusers need lots of understanding, support, and love. But what if your friend is too embarrassed to tell you that he or she has a serious family problem. How can you tell if something is wrong? There may be warning signs like the ones Katie noticed about Sarah. If you can answer yes to more than one of the following questions, your friend may be having trouble at home:

Avoiding a close friend may be a sign of a troubled teen.

- Has your friend stopped inviting you over? There may be a parent at home your friend doesn't want you to see. Or it might be because your friend wants to spend as much time as possible away from home.
- Does your friend make lots of excuses for his or her parent's behavior? Ask yourself how *your* parent would act in a similar situation.
- Does your friend seem depressed? Depressed people often sleep too much, or not sleep at all. They may lose interest in things they once enjoyed. And they may seem not to care about what happens to them. Depression that goes on for a long time may become serious. Listen closely to what your friend is saying. Take it seriously, especially if there is any talk of suicide. He or she may need professional help as well as a good friend.
- Has your friend started to do poorly in school? Sometimes things at home can get so bad that it is impossible for kids even to think about school.
- Has your friend started to drink or experiment with drugs?

If you think a friend is having trouble at home, ask him or her if there's something going on. Be honest. Tell your friend that you are concerned. Be specific about your reasons for being concerned. Your friend may not open up to you right away. He or she may still pretend that everything is fine. Keep trying. Let your friend know that you are always willing to listen.

Showing That You Care

Being a good listener is very important. It's easy to do. Just listen! Let your friend talk about the problem any way he or she wants to. Don't jump in with too many ideas or opinions. Let your friend tell you how he or she feels.

When your friend has finished talking, let him or her know that you care a lot about what is happening. Offer to help in any way you can.

You may want to invite your friend over to your house for a day or so (check with your parents first). You can try to help your friend think of a trusted adult to talk to. Or go with your friend to an Alateen meeting. Doing new things can be scary, even when they are good things to do.

The support of a friend can make a difference. But remember, you can't *solve* your friend's problems. And you can't give up everything in your own life for your friend. If you are trying to help a friend with this problem, let *your* mom or dad know what you are doing. Being a good friend can be hard work. Your parents will want to make sure that you are taking care of yourself, too.

Getting family counseling is the beginning of working out problems and reestablishing healthy relationships.

Chapter 7

Making Things Better for You and Your Parent

I t is possible for a substance-abusing parent to realize he or she needs to stop the abuse. When a parent decides to get help, many things will happen. You may become hopeful about the possibility of getting your parent back. You may get excited about the thought of getting a normal life back.

It is important to remember that even though your parent may decide to get help, his or her recovery will not happen overnight. Your parent may have to go to the hospital for detoxification. Detoxification means getting rid of all the drugs in a person's system. Your parent may be out of the house for a few weeks while they are in rehabilitation. You may feel relieved to have your parent out of the house for a while, even though you miss him or her. It's normal and okay to feel this way.

Your parent needs more than just detoxification to get well. Your mother or father may have recovered from the physical dependency, but he or she must also recover from the psychological dependency. Abusers need to learn to live without drugs. An abuser must learn new patterns and behaviors for dealing with stress and other difficulties they face in daily life.

Most often, a parent will enter a 12-step program, such as Alcoholics Anonymous or Narcotics Anonymous. These meetings are similar to Alateen, Al-Anon, and Nar-Anon, and they give your parent the support he or she needs by surrounding them with other people who have been through similar experiences.

You may be asked to participate in your parent's recovery. Because a parent's abuse affects the entire family, family therapy is often a part of recovery. You may attend sessions with a trained therapist to discuss the problems your parent's substance abuse has caused. This is a positive experience. It will give you a chance to tell your parent how his or her behavior made you feel. Your parent will be in a situation where he or she will be ready to really listen to what you have to say.

Once your parent has made the commitment to stay off drugs or alcohol, there are many things you can do to help him or her.

Let your parent know if you are attending an Alateen or Nar-Anon group and learning about drug abuse. Try to help maintain a healthy atmosphere in the home by including the recovering person in family life. Encourage new interests and participate in activities that your

Teens can help themselves by planning their lives and working toward goals that will bring self-esteem and satisfaction.

Focusing on their own talents and ambitions will enable the children of substance abusers to survive and move forward in life.

parent enjoys. Encourage your parent to see old friends he or she may have avoided because of drug abuse.

Be patient and live one day at a time. Recovery from alcoholism and other drug addiction takes a long time. Try to accept setbacks and relapses with calmness and understanding.

Take Care of Yourself

No matter how much you and your parent love each other, it is possible that your parent won't ever get the help she or he needs. Chemical dependency is a progressive, chronic disease; there is always the possibility of relapse. That will always be painful for you. But you must take charge of your own life. You have choices. You can make a better life for yourself even if your parent's life goes on as before. Your parent's disease does not have to destroy you. Set your own goals. Plan for your future by doing the best you can now.

You Can Succeed

Bill Clinton's stepfather was an abusive alcoholic. Clinton's brother was a drug addict. And yet, Bill Clinton grew up to be a top scholar and to attend the finest schools. He became governor of Arkanas, was elected president of the United States in 1992, and was reelected in 1996. Keep him in mind as you make your way through these difficult years. Clinton did not choose to remain a victim. He moved beyond self-pity. He became a survivor instead. He believed in his own ability—and he went ahead to accomplish great things. So can you!

A Note from the Author

I am also the child of a substance abuser.
My father was an alcoholic most of my childhood. He stopped drinking when I was 18
years old. I was often very sad while I was
growing up. Sometimes I was scared. Sometimes I was mad. Sometimes I was very
embarrassed. I never told anyone what was
going on in my house. Once, when I was a
grown-up, I found out that a friend of mine
also had an alcoholic father. It was such a
relief to talk to him! I found out that he had
felt just the way I had, and that I was not
alone! How I wished I could have talked to
someone when I was younger and trying to
cope.

I am living proof that you can survive this.
I want you to survive this, too. Get all the
help you can. Believe in yourself. Look
forward to the rest of your life. And don't
overlook the positive things in your life—
good friends, ice cream, opening day of the
baseball season. There is joy to be had, and
you deserve it!

Glossary—*Explaining New Words*

chronic Lasting a long time or recurring.

codependent A person affected by someone else's chemical dependence.

dependent When you rely on another person or substance for support.

depressant A substance that slows down the systems in the body.

drunk Condition that occurs when too much alcohol is taken into the body. Drunk people cannot think clearly or act normally.

enabler Someone who protects a substance abuser from the harmful effects of his or her addiction. Person who helps another to remain dependent on a drug.

hallucinogen A substance that causes the user to see, hear, feel, and sense things that are not real.

"high" or "stoned" Describing someone who is on drugs.

narcotic Drug that is intended to ease pain.

progressive Continuing by successive steps.

recovery Healing time after substance abuser stops using drugs.

relapse A falling back into a former condition after it seemed to be improved.

self-esteem A person's feelings about himself or herself.

stimulant Drug that increases heart rate and pulse; often gives user greater energy.

substance-abuse professional Person who has special education and experience in the disease of substance abuse and who is trained to help substance abusers get better.

substance abuser Someone who uses drugs and/or alcohol so much that it causes problems for himself or herself and for others.

symptom Physical sign of a medical problem.

Where to Go for Help

There are many organizations and people you can call to get help. Talk to a family member, guidance counselor, teacher, social worker, priest, minister, rabbi, or any other trusted adult. You can contact one of these groups, which are made up of people with problems just like yours.

Al-Anon/Alateen Family Group
   Headquarters, Inc.
1600 Corporate Landing Parkway
Virginia Beach, VA 23454
(800) 356-9996 (general info)
(800) 344-2666 (meeting info)
Web site: http://www.al-anon.
   alateen.org

The Children of Alcoholics
   Foundation
555 Madison Avenue, 20th Floor
New York, NY 10022
(800) 359-COAF
e-mail: coafdn@aol.com

Nar-Anon/Narateen Family
   Groups
P.O. Box 2562
Palos Verdes, CA 90274
(310) 547-5800

National Association for
   Children of Alcoholics
11426 Rockville Pike, Suite 100
Rockville, MD 20852
(301) 468-0985
(888) 554-COAS
Web site: http://www.health.org/
   NACOA

In Canada:
Al-Anon/Alateen
National Public Information
   Canada (NPIC)
P.O. Box 6433
Station J
Ottawa, ON K2A 3Y6
(613) 722-1830

Alcoholics Anonymous
#502, Intergroup Office
234 Englington Avenue E.
Toronto, ON M4P 1K5
(416) 487-5591

Alcohol and Drug Dependency
   Information and Counseling
   Services (ADDICS)
#2, 2471 1/2 Portage Avenue
Winnipeg, MB R3J 0N6
(204) 831-1999

Narcotics Anonymous
P.O. Box 7500
Station A
Tornto, ON M5W 1P9
(416) 691-9519

For Further Reading

Alateen—Hope for Children of Alcoholics. New York: Al-Anon Family Group Headquarters, Inc. 1989.

Leite, Evelyn, and Espeland, Pamela. *Different Like Me: A Book for Teens Who Worry about Their Parents' Use of Alcohol/Drugs*. Minneapolis: Johnson Institute Books, 1987.

McFarland, Rhoda. *Drugs and Your Parents*, rev. ed. New York: The Rosen Publishing Group, 1997.

Seixas, Judith S. *Living with a Parent Who Takes Drugs*. New York: Greenwillow Books, 1989.

Challenging Reading

Minkler, Meredith. *Grandmothers as Caregivers: Raising Children of the Crack Cocaine Epidemic*. Newbury Park, CA: Sage Publications, 1993.

Index

A

addiction to drugs
  how it happens, 13–14
  how to recognize, 12–13
Al-Anon, 45, 54
Alateen, 44, 51, 54
alcohol, as a drug, 8, 12, 13, 14,
    16
Alcoholics Anonymous, 54
alcoholism, 25, 57
amphetamines, 16

B

barbiturates, 12

C

changes
  in behavior, 15, 18–20
  in parenting, 22, 24
  physical and mental, 16–20
children of drug abusers, 6–9,
    13–14, 23–24, 27–33, 34–35,
    37–38, 40, 45
cocaine, 8, 12, 16
codependency, 37–38, 40
coping (with drug-abusing
    parents), 28–29, 32–33,
    41–42
crack, 8, 12, 13, 16
cycle (of addiction), 34–35

D

denial, 35
depressants, 8, 12, 16, 18

depression, 50
drug abuse
  as a disease, 6, 8, 24–25, 53, 54
  effects of, 15, 16, 18, 20, 27–29
  goals in surviving, 54, 57
  warning signs and symptoms
    of, 8, 13, 22, 48, 50–51
drugs
  definition of, 11
  illegal, 12
  legal, 11

E

enabling, 37–38, 40

F

families and addiction, 14, 20,
    22, 24

G

genetics (role in drug
    addiction), 14, 34–35

H

hallucinogens, 12, 18
help
  getting, 9, 14, 25, 41, 42, 44–45
  giving (to a friend or parent),
    47–48, 50–51, 53–54, 57
heroin, 12, 13, 18

L

LSD, 12, 18

About the Author
Frannie Shuker-Haines is a free-lance writer currently living in Ann Arbor, Michigan. She specializes in writing about parenting and child rearing.

Acknowledgments and Photo Credits
Cover photo by Dick Smolinski. Photograph on page 10 © AP/Wide World Photos; all other photos by Mary Lauzon.

DATE DUE
